National Park Explorers

BIG BEND

by Lori Dittmer

CREATIVE EDUCATION · CREATIVE PAPERBACKS

TABLE OF CONTENTS

Green Gulch in the Chisos Mountains (left); a red fox (right)

WELCOME TO BIG BEND NATIONAL PARK!

Look through the window of the Chisos
Mountains! It frames the **desert** below. A lonely
group of cottonwood trees marks an **oasis**.

5

Big Bend is in southwestern Texas. It became a national park in 1944. It is known for its mountains and canyons.

6

★ Big Bend National Park
■ Texas

The Chisos Mountains (above) are along the Rio Grande (right).

A BEND IN THE RIVER

The Rio Grande marks the southern edge of
Big Bend. This river separates Texas and Mexico.
The park was named for the river's sharp curve.

People hike the park's many trails. The desert is hot! It is cooler in the mountains. Trees can grow there. Canyons cut through the mountains.

A hiker looks up at a century plant.

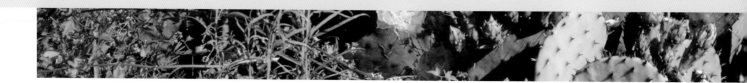

ADAPTABLE LIFE

More than 40 kinds of cacti grow in Big Bend.
Mesquite roots reach down 160 feet (48.8 m)
to find water. In early spring, bluebonnets
blanket the land.

About 450 kinds of birds take shelter here. Rattlesnakes slither over the sand. If you see one, go the other way! **Javelinas** munch prickly pear cactus. Foxes and bobcats hunt at night.

Javelinas (above); a cactus wren on a cholla (right)

LOOK TO THE STARS

More than 300,000 people visit Big Bend each year. It is a good place for stargazing. Stars shine brightly in the dark sky.

Some visitors take canoes or rafts on the Rio Grande. Others hike or ride horses on trails. Bird-watching is also popular in Big Bend.

Canoeists traveling through the Santa Elena canyon rest on the sandbars.

Bring lots of water. Tell the **rangers** where you are going. They can teach you how to stay safe in the park.

Most animals hide in the shade during the day.

20

Activity

Materials needed:

3 wet paper towels

Sheet-cake pan

2 paper clips

Sheet of waxed paper
slightly bigger than a
paper towel

Step 1: Lay one paper towel flat on the pan.

Step 2: Roll up the second paper towel. Set it on the pan.

Step 3: Lay the last paper towel on top of the waxed paper. (Waxed paper is similar to the skin of a cactus.) Roll together and hold in place with the paper clips. Set on the pan.

Step 4: After 24 hours, unroll the paper towels. Compare the three. Are any of them still damp?

22

Glossary

cacti — plants with thick stems and sharp spines that can survive without much water

canyons — deep valleys with rocky walls

desert — hot, dry land that gets little rain

javelinas — piglike animals found from the southwestern U.S. through South America

oasis — a spot in a desert where water is found and plants can grow

rangers — people who take care of a park

Read More

National Geographic Kids. *National Parks Guide USA Centennial Edition: The Most Amazing Sights, Scenes, and Cool Activities from Coast to Coast!* Washington, D.C.: National Geographic, 2016.

Robson, Gary D. *Who Pooped in the Park? Big Bend National Park: Scat and Tracks for Kids.* Helena, Mont.: Farcountry Press, 2006.

Websites

National Geographic Kids: National Parks
https://kids.nationalgeographic.com/explore/nature/national-parks/
Learn about the national parks of the United States, and take a quiz.

National Park Service: Big Bend National Park for Kids
https://www.nps.gov/bibe/learn/kidsyouth/index.htm
Find out how to become a junior ranger, and download an activity book.

Index

Published by Creative Education and Creative Paperbacks
P.O. Box 227, Mankato, Minnesota 56002
Creative Education and Creative Paperbacks are imprints of
The Creative Company
www.thecreativecompany.us

Design by Christine Vanderbeek
Production by Dana Cheit
Art direction by Rita Marshall
Printed in the United States of America

Photographs by Alamy (Heather Drake, George H.H. Huey,
Efrain Padro, Rolf Nussbaumer Photography, Tom Till),
Dreamstime (Steven Prorak, Wisconsinart), Getty Images (Kick
Images), iStockphoto (adogslifephoto, CrackerClips, cretolamna,
DenisTangneyJr, dhughes9, jerryhopman, JKSMIRTH,
kellyvandellen, mandj98, moonisblack, phleum, sdbower, va103,
Wildnerdpix), Shutterstock (Tarchyshnik Andrei; Tom Baker; Chin-
Hong, Cheah)

Library of Congress Cataloging-in-Publication Data
Names: Dittmer, Lori, author. • Title: Big Bend / Lori Dittmer.
Series: National park explorers. • Includes bibliographical references
and index. • *Summary:* A young explorer's introduction to Texas's Big
Bend National Park, covering its desert landscape, plants, animals
such as javelinas, and activities such as stargazing.
Identifiers: ISBN 978-1-64026-066-5 (hardcover) / ISBN 978-1-
62832-654-3 (pbk) / ISBN 978-1-64000-182-4 (eBook)
This title has been submitted for CIP processing under LCCN
2018938989.

CCSS: RI.1.1, 2, 3, 4, 5, 6, 7, 10; RI.2.1, 2, 3, 5, 6, 7; RI.3.1, 3, 5, 7;
RF.1.1, 3, 4; RF.2.4

First Edition HC 9 8 7 6 5 4 3 2 1
First Edition PBK 9 8 7 6 5 4 3 2 1